Groundhog

Backyard Animals

Heather Kissock

AV2

www.openlightbox.com

AV2

Step 1
Go to **www.openlightbox.com**

Step 2
Enter this unique code
LRHYS1EF4

Step 3
Explore your interactive eBook!

AV2 is optimized for use on any device

Your interactive eBook comes with...

- Read — **Audio** Listen to the entire book read aloud
- **Videos** Watch informative video clips
- **Weblinks** Gain additional information for research
- **Try This!** Complete activities and hands-on experiments
- **Key Words** Study vocabulary, and complete a matching word activity
- **Quizzes** Test your knowledge
- **Slideshows** View images and captions
- **Share** Share titles within your Learning Management System (LMS) or Library Circulation System
- **Citation** Create bibliographical references following APA, CMOS, and MLA styles

This title is part of our AV2 digital subscription

1-Year K–5 Subscription
ISBN 978-1-7911-3320-7

Access hundreds of AV2 titles with our digital subscription.
Sign up for a FREE trial at **www.openlightbox.com/trial**

The digital components of this book are guaranteed to stay active for at least five years from the date of publication.

Groundhog

Backyard Animals

CONTENTS

Meet the groundhog.

She likes to dig holes in the ground.

She digs underground with her sharp claws.

Her sharp claws help her climb trees.

She lives with her mother when she is young.

When she is young, her mother keeps her warm.

She stays underground in the winter.

In the winter, she spends most of her time asleep.

She likes to lie in the sun when summer comes.

When summer comes, she finds food to eat.

When talking, she often makes whistling sounds.

Whistling sounds warn others of danger.

She can run quickly with her strong legs.

With her strong legs, she can also swim.

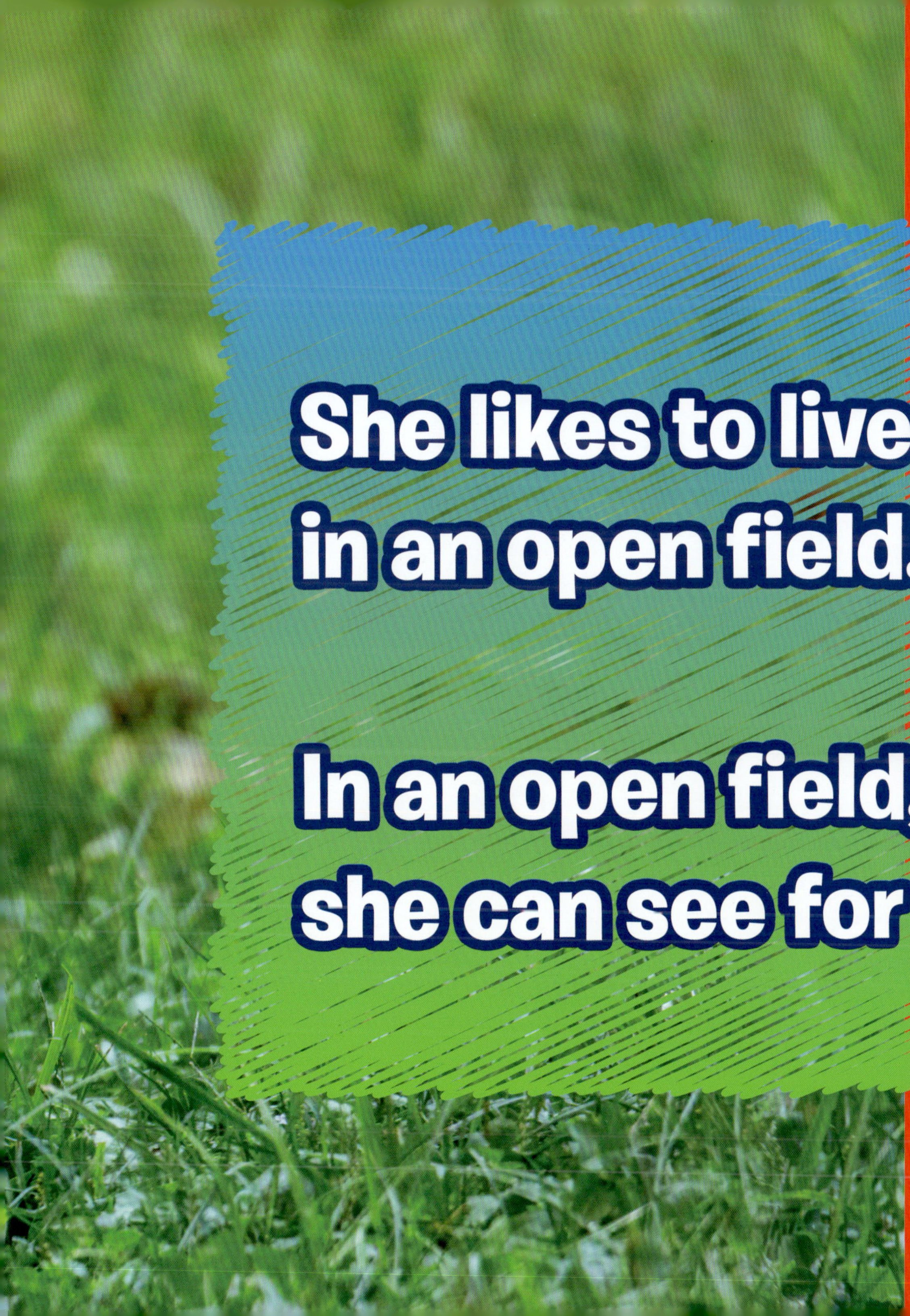

She likes to live
in an open field.

In an open field,
she can see for miles.

If you meet the groundhog, she might be surprised. She may run away.

If you meet the groundhog, stay away.

Groundhog Facts

These pages provide more detail about the interesting facts found in the book. They are intended to be used by adults as a learning support to help young readers round out their knowledge of each animal featured in the *Backyard Animals* series.

Pages 4–5

Groundhogs like to dig holes. The groundhog is the largest member of the squirrel family. It can measure up to 20 inches (51 centimeters) in length and weigh up to 13 pounds (6 kilograms). Groundhogs are known for creating their homes, called burrows, by digging into the ground. A groundhog can move more than 700 pounds (318 kg) of dirt to make one burrow.

Pages 6–7

A groundhog has sharp claws. The claws are also curved, allowing the groundhog to use them like shovels when digging the burrow. A groundhog will use its claws to defend itself against predators, such as coyotes and bobcats. The groundhog may also use its claws to climb a tree in an effort to escape a predator.

Pages 8–9

Groundhogs live with their mother when they are young. A female groundhog typically gives birth to three to six young, called kits. The newborn kits have no fur and cannot see or hear. They rely on their mother for food and warmth. The kits grow fast, however, and will leave their mother at about 2 months of age to begin life on their own.

Pages 10–11

Groundhogs stay in their burrows over the winter months. Groundhogs are true hibernators. This means they sleep through the winter, waking only occasionally. A groundhog will not eat during hibernation. As a result, it can lose up to one-quarter of its weight during this time. A groundhog survives using fat from food it has eaten in the months before winter.

Pages 12–13

In the summer, groundhogs spend much of their time feeding. They are herbivores, which means they eat mainly plants. Their diet can include grasses, leaves, bark, and fruits. They may also eat insects from time to time. When not feeding, they either sleep or take time to bask in the warmth of the sunlight.

Pages 14–15

Groundhogs make sounds to communicate. One of their best-known sounds is a whistle, which they use to alert other groundhogs of a nearby threat. Groundhogs are sometimes called "whistle pigs" for this reason. A groundhog can also vocalize with grunts, chirps, barks, and hisses.

Pages 16–17

Groundhogs can move fast for their size. A groundhog can run at speeds up to 10 miles (16 kilometers) per hour. However, these speeds can only be attained in short bursts, mainly when the animal has been frightened. Groundhogs typically move at a much slower pace. A groundhog's strong legs are also helpful in the water, allowing it to swim in search of food or to escape a predator.

Pages 18–19

Groundhogs like to live in open areas. They are found mostly in fields and on forest edges. These habitats give them easy access to food sources. The openness also allows them to watch for danger. Groundhogs can often be seen standing on their back legs, surveying their territory for interlopers.

Pages 20–21

Groundhogs are rarely dangerous to humans. If a person comes close, they are most likely to scurry underground. Groundhogs may sometimes build burrows in urban areas, including backyards. This can lead to increased human contact. In these cases, it is important to give a groundhog space and seek professional advice to remove it from the area.

KEY WORDS

Research has shown that as much as 65 percent of all written material published in English is made up of 300 words. These 300 words cannot be taught using pictures or learned by sounding them out. They must be recognized by sight. This book contains 44 common sight words to help young readers improve their reading fluency and comprehension. This book also teaches young readers several important content words. These words are paired with pictures to aid in learning and improve understanding.

Page	Sight Words First Appearance
4	in, likes, she, the, to
6	her, with
7	help, trees
8	is, keeps, lives, mother, when, young
10	a, home
11	most, of, time
12	comes
13	and, eat, finds, food, leaves
14	makes, often, sounds
15	others
16	can, run
17	also
19	an, for, miles, open, see
20	away, be, if, may, might, you

Page	Content Words First Appearance
4	ground, groundhog, holes
6	claws
10	bathroom, main entrance, nursery, sleep chamber, tunnels, turnaround chamber, winter
12	summer, sun
13	bark, berries, diet, ferns, grasses, twigs
15	danger
16	legs
19	field

Published by Lightbox Learning Inc.
276 5th Avenue, Suite 704 #917
New York, NY 10001
Website: www.openlightbox.com

Library of Congress Control Number: 2023931930

ISBN 978-1-7911-5527-8 (hardcover)
ISBN 978-1-7911-5528-5 (softcover)
ISBN 978-1-7911-5529-2 (multi-user eBook)

Printed in Guangzhou, China
1 2 3 4 5 6 7 8 9 0 27 26 25 24 23

022023
100922

Project Coordinator: Heather Kissock **Designer:** Jean Rodriguez

The publisher acknowledges Alamy, Shutterstock, Bigstock, and Dreamstime as the primary image suppliers for this title.